D1536920

Proudly printed in the United States of America

To contact the author about speaking engagements or for more information please visit www.happyenterprises.com

Published By:
Spirit Books Publications

CHOOSE HAPPY

Your

GO-TO-GUIDE

For

Living a Happier life

Introduction:

When I was in elementary school I had an arts and crafts assignment to create a book out of construction paper and crayons and write what makes me happy. I called it Happiness is...and each page listed something different. I remember it so vividly. It could easily be my favorite school project of all time. It was fun, easy and made me happy. It was fun because it allowed me to think about happy things. It was easy because all I had to do was think of things I like and write them down, and it made me happy because I now had a book to look at of all the things I like. Out of the entire class, my book was the biggest by far. I just kept writing things that made me happy. As I think back to the things I wrote...ice cream, the swing set in my backyard, etc. I realize that they made me happy because they were connected to the people that make me happy. My parents and I would go out for ice cream to enjoy family time, my friends and I would laugh and play for hours on the swing set. Not too much has changed. Admittedly, I try to limit my ice cream and haven't been on a swing set in quite a while but it is still spending time with the special people in my life that makes me the most happy. Oh, and the assignment? It was proudly displayed on my family's kitchen refrigerator...which made me very happy :)

About the Author:

Jill Liberman is a former talk show host and media veteran of many years. Choose Happy is her third book.

JILL LIBERMAN

Dedication

This book is dedicated to Stan and Adam who give me a reason to be happy every day.

Table of Contents

"There are so many reasons to be happy"

Oh Brother!

My brother and his wife recently had a baby. My family and I went to visit my new nephew and took turns guessing what the baby would be when he grows up. His career ranged from Olympic swimmer (my sister's guess) to an architect. Finally someone asked my brother what *he* would like his son to be. Without any hesitation, my brother was quick to answer. "Happy" he said.

Choose Happy

My friend's mother told me about an essay her high school aged granddaughter wrote called "Happiness is a Choice." What is special about the paper is that the young girl wrote it shortly after her mother, my friend from elementary school, died of ovarian cancer. People used to ask my friend if she put toothpicks in her cheeks because her dimples were so deep. Even while going through her illness she **chose** to be happy.

"It isn't what you have, or who you are, or where you are, or what you are doing that makes you happy or unhappy. It is what you think about."

Dale Carnegie

"I eat cake Every Day...because it's Somebody's birthday somewhere"

Celebrate every day

It's not that...

Let's talk about what happiness *isn't*. Happiness isn't an event. A family friend recently got married. After months of planning for the big day, she said to me she doesn't have anything to look forward to anymore. A healthy young woman who is starting a life with her new groom...lucky enough to begin and end her day with someone who loves her, but she looks to occasions to find happiness. Graduation, marriage, birth of a baby, promotions at work are all exciting events worthy of looking forward to and celebrating. How many of those events do we usually experience in a lifetime? Three? Four? Maybe five? Does that mean we are only going to be happy five times in our life? Of course not. We all have reasons to be happy every day. We need to recognize them and live in the moment, not for a specific moment. Happiness is not an event.

"Happiness is an attitude. We either make ourselves miserable, or happy and strong. The amount of work is the same."

— Francesca Reigler

What Happiness isn't

Happiness is not a material thing. There is a saying "Money can't buy happiness, but it sure can help!" I know people with lots and lots of really nice things...who are not happy. They keep buying more nice things...still, not happy. Then I know people with very few material belongings and they are very happy. Don't misunderstand me. A person can have expensive toys **and** be happy. I'm just saying the toys are not delivering the happiness. Only one thing creates happiness, your mind.

Do you mind?

The mind is very powerful. Our life is a result of the way we think. I graduated college with a degree in psychology and for a few years was a behavior therapist. Many of my clients came to see me because they were unhappy with their weight. They knew they should be exercising but were not. I helped them realize something about themselves that made all the difference. It was all in their mind. When I asked them what words come immediately to mind when they think of exercise the answers were all similar: sweat, pain, no time, even... yuck! Well, no wonder you're not doing it, I told them. Who wants to do anything associated with pain, sweat and yuck! When they began thinking of exercising in a positive way, and associating it with words like weight loss, feeling great, energy, good health, longevity and looking amazing, every single one of my clients reached his or her weight loss goal!! When you change the way you think, you change your life.

"MOST PEOPLE ARE AS
HAPPY AS THEY MAKE UP
THEIR MINDS TO BE"

"Happy People don't have the best of everything. They make the best of everything"

There are 7 Days in a Week, and Someday Isn't one of them

When do most people start a diet? Tomorrow! When we put something off until "tomorrow" it is basically a no commitment-commitment. We appease ourselves by agreeing to do something but are not taking any action. So, we commit but don't. See how that works? How many times have you or someone you know said "I'll be happy when____" (You fill in the blank). I'll be happy when I find a job, I'll be happy when my kid cleans his room, I'll be happy when someone invents diet chocolate...start today. There is a saying life is about the journey, not the destination. The same is true for happiness. Enjoy the journey.

Don't Force...Enforce

When I was little my cousin came to visit. He was so excited to share what they did in school that day. He asked all of us to think of anything *but* an elephant for the next 2 minutes. Easy, I thought. You know what I thought about? Elephants! I tried again...still elephants! From time to time I try that exercise, and those elephants continue to be there. We can't force our thoughts. I remember my friend's husband was throwing her a surprise birthday party. I am a great secret keeper. They both came to my house the day before the party. All I could think about was not to mention the party. I could hardly form a sentence without thinking about not mentioning the party. As they were leaving I said see you at the party!!! Fortunately I was able to talk my way out of it so she thought I was referring to something else. You can't force your thoughts. If you bully yourself into being happy it won't work. Choosing happy is a time you don't want the force to be with you.

"It's not about forcing happiness; it's about not letting the sadness win"

"BEING HAPPY DOESN'T MEAN EVERYTHING IS PERFECT. IT MEANS YOU'VE DECIDED TO LOOK BEYOND THE IMPERFECTION"

Perfectly Happy

Being happy is not about living a perfect life. You may not have a lot of money in the bank. Perhaps you just ended a relationship. Maybe those extra pounds aren't coming off quickly enough. Your health may be compromised. We all have something. Don't let challenges interfere with the way you look at the world. You always have a **choice** to be happy.

Mr. Right

Do you know people who argue for so long they don't even remember what they were arguing about? I know a couple that argue about *everything*. He can start a story with "My cousin Susie" and she will interrupt with "she's not your cousin, she's your second cousin"...the poor man can not finish a sentence without being interrupted. Married couples know the two most important words to a happy relationship are "yes, dear". If you ask me, I'd rather be happy than right.

"Everything is either an opportunity to grow or an obstacle to keep you from growing. You get to choose."

"If you want to fly you need to give up the stuff that weighs you down"

Up, Up and Away!

Sometimes, less is more. When I write, I re read my words and eliminate any thing I feel isn't necessary. After all, the reader wants to get to the point, no need for extra stuff. When I travel, I pack what I need. Who wants to carry extra baggage? The same goes for being happy. Surround yourself with people who lift you up and things that cheer you up...and you won't feel down. Eliminate all clutter in your life... whether it is in the form of people, things or negative thoughts.

Silver Linings can be Golden

Some people appear to have the golden touch. Those are the people who find the silver lining. They look like good things come their way because they focus on the positive. Concentrating on the good is different from denying or ignoring the "not so good". They see the best in situations. They recognize challenges are only temporary. Happy people use setbacks as opportunities

"Tough times don't last, tough people do"

"When it rains look for rainbows, when it's dark look for stars"

Lemonade

We all know the saying when life gives us lemons, make lemonade. I know so many situations where an apparent obstacle turned into an exciting opportunity. When I worked in television, my friend and former co-worker was ready for a change and new challenge so he embarked in a career in an entirely different industry. He was willing to start his new job in an entry level position so he could learn the ropes. One day, quite unexpectedly, the owner of the company called a meeting and announced the business was closing its doors...that day. My friend, and all the other employees were out of work, with no paycheck on the way, and no warning. After allowing himself to go through the necessary emotions, he got back into the mode of positive thinking. He loved his new industry and learned a lot in the time he was with the company. He believed in himself and in the need for what the company offered. So...he made lemonade. He started his own business in that same field. He began very small and grew *his* company into an international success. What he thought was the worst day of his life turned out to be one of the best. Gotta love lemonade!!.

You Got This

Certain things are best left to a professional. Leaky faucet? Call a plumber. Looking for happiness? It's all you! Happiness truly is a choice. *Your* choice. You will be surprised how much happier every day is when you simply make the decision to choose happiness.

"Happiness is an inside job. Don't give anyone else that much power over your life"

"The past is a place of reference not a place of residence"

The Present is your Present

It is so easy to use your past as an excuse for something in your life that makes you unhappy. I've heard people say it's no wonder they are overweight, they were heavy as a child. The list goes on and on. Interestingly, many leading entertainers, journalists, business people and politicians have less than perfect pasts and went on to have happy, fulfilling lives. They used the obstacles as fuel to succeed. More importantly, they left the past where it belongs, behind them.

Dream On

Everything starts with a dream, a vision. A store I like to visit has a sign hanging in the entrance that says "Don't Dream Your Life, Live Your Dreams". The owner is living hers. She wanted to start her own business and did. Go for your dreams.

"Whenever you think you are rejected from something good you are actually being redirected to something better"

"Look closely at the present life you are constructing. It should look like the future you are dreaming"

Thanks for the Memories

Before the onset of selfies, I was the one usually missing from photos because I was *taking* them. Creating memories is important to me. I was having dinner with a friend who was talking about her aunt who passed away at the age of 93. I asked her to tell me about her aunt. "She wore a lot of perfume" my friend said. I sure hope people remember me for much more than my perfume. While I'm sure her aunt was a lovely lady, that comment made me think. How do you want people to think of you when you meet? There have been times I see people being introduced who have met before, one remembers, the other doesn't. When you choose happy, people remember you. "Seek to be worth knowing rather than well known".

"Each day we make deposits in the memory banks for our children"

"THE DIFFERENCE
BETWEEN STUMBLING
BLOCKS AND STEPPING
STONES IS HOW YOU USE
THEM"

Your Favorite program

You need to program the way you think into positive mode because when you believe, you will succeed. Forgot all the reasons why not and think of why something *will* work. When you believe you can, you will, because you are already halfway there.

Make No Bones about It

Happy people share certain qualities. They believe in themselves enough not to have to care what others think or say and they don't take themselves too seriously.

"The more you love your decisions the less you need others to love them"

"To thrive in life you need 3 bones: a wishbone, a backbone and a funny bone"

"There is a difference between giving up and knowing when you have had enough"

Timing is everything.

When my aunt resigned from her job the first thing she said was she should have done that a long time ago. She looks ten years younger. She smiles more. She was unhappy in her job for YEARS. One of the easiest ways to be happy is to get rid of what makes you sad.

Be a Swimmer

Remember when the phone rang and you were offered you your dream job? How about the time you woke up and those ten pounds you wanted to lose were magically gone? Oh- and the time your soul mate was waiting for you at your doorstep. If we want to live the life we dream about, we need to create our own opportunities. Don't wait...create.

"If your ship doesn't come in, swim out to meet it!"

"GET DOWN ON YOUR KNEES AND BE THANKFUL YOU'RE STILL ON YOUR FEET"

Thanksgiving

Without a doubt, Thanksgiving is my favorite
holiday. It is time with family and good friends
(ok..and good food). Pardon the pun, but I am
especially corny on that day. I make sure to tell the
people I love I am thankful for them. The rest of the
year I continue to be grateful for my life and the
people in it. Gratitude is a big part of being happy.

"You cannot always have happiness, but you can always give happiness"

What gives?

Not too long ago I ran into an acquaintance of mine. She greeted me with a warm hug and huge smile. She then went on to thank me. For what? I asked. I heard she was going through a difficult time and I sent her a note to let her know I was thinking of her. Until she mentioned it I had even forgotten I sent it. The point is, often what we think of as little things are truly the big things. One of the biggest things we can do is bring happiness to another person. Be generous in your deeds.

Figure it out

I am devoted to a life of healthy living and well-being. However, I do not belong to a gym...I do not even like to sweat. I found a way to exercise regularly that still met my "requirements". How? I arm myself with songs that make me happy, hit "play", turn up the volume, and walk(ok... sing, too) I look forward to it, am happy while I'm doing it and feel great afterwards. Happy people do not find excuses, they find a way.

"You need to be proactive, carve out time in your schedule, and take responsibility for being the healthiest person you can be - no one else is going to do it for you".

Mehmet Oz

Did you hear the one about....

When I wrote my first book, I was invited to be a guest on a well - known morning talk show. The make- up artist put false eyelashes on me. Immediately after that interview I had a meeting with another network to discuss a television special. In the cab on the way there, something became unglued. No, not me... the false eyelashes. I'm pretty sure that having a row of eyelashes dangling across your cheek is not on the list of how to make a good first impression. The television special didn't happen, but I did walk away with a good story. Sometimes the best thing to do is laugh, knowing what didn't quite work out may be a good story one day. We don't see things as they are, we see them as we are. A happy person sees the positive.

"Happiness is mind over matter. If you don't mind, it doesn't matter"

Guilty Pleasure

I think people believe they are supposed to feel guilty when they do things that make them happy. Have you noticed that labels on low calorie desserts say "Guilt Free" implying we should feel guilty when we eat dessert. I enjoy my chocolate...and refuse to feel anything but happy when I do. Drop the guilt. You deserve to be happy.

"HAPPINESS IS HAVING YOUR CAKE AND EATING IT TOO"

"Treat everyone with kindness and respect – not because they are nice, but because you are"

What's up?

I'm not big on heavy lifting but show me something that lifts *for* me, count me in. For example, clothes that lift and creams that help fight gravity, bring it. Same is true for people. We *gravitate* to people and things that are uplifting.

Be an Environmentalist

Happy people live in positive environments. When I say live, I am not talking about their physical neighborhood, I mean emotionally. A positive space. I once stayed at a spa that had a special room called the relaxation room. It was not anything fancy, just a room with a plant and a sign that said relaxation room. But it _was_ relaxing...and empty. Just me and the plant. Find your relaxation room. (plant optional).

"WHENEVER I FEEL SAD, I JUST GO TO MY HAPPY PLACE. THE FRIDGE."

"You yourself as much as anybody in the entire universe deserve your love and affection." — Buddha

You are the star of your Life

There used to be a popular soap opera called "One Life to Live". It was filled with drama. Millions of people tuned in to see the action in the fictional city of LLanview. We have the lead role in our lives. It's our show. We get one life, starring us. Only one person has the power to make you happy in your life : YOU.

See the Value

Choosing happy is all about the way you think and the way you see yourself. Not how others see you. Happy people know that their value doesn't decrease based on someone's inability to see their worth. If you are in a situation where someone is trying to devalue you, walk away.

"Sometimes walking away is a step forward"

"A smile increases your face value"

Doodly-do

I grew up pre computer age. In the "old days" we had notebooks in school. When classes were less than exciting, we would doodle in the notebooks to pass the time. Most of us drew hearts on every page. Studying psychology we learned that we can learn a lot about a person from what he or she draws. If you were to doodle today- would your notebook have smiley faces?

Take Care

 I am aware that I have made reference to sweets more than once in this book. Food is a part of my life. I even named my dog after a food. Healthy living is a priority to me as well. I believe happiness and health go hand in hand. Happiness is a lot easier to achieve when we feel well physically. A healthy body and healthy mind go hand in hand. They go together like, well, peanut butter and jelly.

"Take Care of your body. It's the only place you have to live "

"When you smile about the life you live, you end up living a life worth smiling about"

Happiness isn't found in a turkey

One year for the holidays I invited 30 guests to join us for dinner. An hour before they arrived every house on my street lost electrical power. No lights, no air conditioning, no hot food. We still had a very happy holiday. Happiness isn't in the turkey, it is in the friends and family enjoying each other's company....even in the dark

Is there a pill for that?

We live in a world of instant gratification. Instant coffee, instant oatmeal...I wrote a book called Instant Sexy. When my son was in middle school I went to pick him up from his friend's house. I didn't know the friend's mother very well. When she answered the door, I asked her how her day was. She enthusiastically responded that she spent an hour connected to a very expensive body-vibrating device. No kidding. She heard it was a way to lose weight. "Sounds interesting" I said and left it at that. As my son and I walked back to my car I wondered if I was missing something. She paid money to be attached to an electronic device that would exercise *for* her? I hate to be the bearer of bad news (especially in a book about being happy) but some things you just have to do for yourself. Choosing happy is one of them.

"Much happiness is overlooked because it doesn't cost anything."

Your life...Unplugged

Ahhh...the good old days. Remember face to face interaction? Or when we actually called people instead of sent a text? The other day someone texted me an acronym I had never seen before. Thankfully for any old school, slightly technology challenged person like me, you can google the term and learn the meaning. So I did. I found a page that translated slang. As I scrolled down the page getting an education in today's slang, at the bottom of the list I saw WYMM? Will you marry me!! Seriously. Now I'm thinking even a happy person would NOT be happy to get a marriage proposal arrive through a text. Take time to get unplugged and as you disconnect your tablets and smart phones, make time to re connect with friends and family. I never did find the acronym I was looking for, must have been a typo. LOL.

"Good things often happen when you least expect it."

"Nobody can make you feel badly without your permission"

Permission

We are taught from a young age to ask permission. Growing up, I needed permission to be excused from the dinner table. In school we needed permission to get a drink of water or to use the rest room. Give yourself permission to be happy.

Smile, baby

Some people just know how to make babies smile. My
mother is one of those people. My husband is that way with
animals. People...and animals instinctively sense warmth and
kindness. It is more than the words we say
that cause people...and animals to feel comfortable.
Sometimes we don't need to say anything at all. It doesn't
matter if it is a baby, a dog, or a baby dog...all living things
respond well to kindness.

"EVERYONE SMILES IN THE SAME LANGUAGE."

"There is always someone that is more than happy who has less than what you have."

How are you...dare I ask

The first words we usually say when we see or speak to someone we know is "How are you?"...unless it is a certain someone. I know a person always quick to answer with a long list of aches, pains and ailments....and then goes on to say "but it could be worse." She finds *something* to complain about...and follows it with "not that I'm complaining". To the contrary, I just learned that someone I know contracted shingles. I called to see how he is doing and he never even mentioned not feeling well. I know that he is in pain and not able to sleep, but it is not his nature to focus on that. His spirits are great. We hung up and he called me about 5 minutes later. "I forgot to tell you something. I went to the doctor this morning. He said I have shingles." He is a perfect example of a person choosing to be happy.

Picture This

A frown is just a smile turned upside down. Even negative situations can have positive consequences if you choose to see them. Losing a job, for example. Not pleasant. Suddenly you find yourself unemployed. You can look at the down side or focus on the positive such as the friends and contacts you made while you were there. And, if you didn't get along with your coworkers, it is for the best you parted ways. Choose to find the good in the situation. The skills you gained from the job. How the next job could be the one your dream job. Maybe leaving is a sign to pursue a career you always wanted.

"Life is like photography. You need the negatives to develop"

Half and Half

Are you a glass is half empty or half full person? Do you see Wednesdays as the week is half over or half the week is still left? Both are correct. The way you see things directly impacts the way you see your life .The difference between choosing to be happy or not is how you see things. Happy people automatically see the glass as half full.

"WE CAN COMPLAIN BECAUSE ROSE BUSHES HAVE THORNS OR REJOICE BECAUSE THORN BUSHES HAVE ROSES"

Abraham Lincoln

"Happiness radiates like the fragrance from a flower, and draws all good things toward you."

Maharishi Mahesh Yogi

Everyone Can Draw

You do not have to be an artist to draw people. We either draw people toward us or away. Happy people attract good things into their lives.

Show Emotion

Humans experience many emotions. Some are healthy, some are not. Living a happy life means getting rid of negative emotions such as anger and learning to limit emotions such as fear.

"Life is short, live it. Love is rare, grab it. Anger is bad, dump it. Fear is awful, face it. Memories are sweet, cherish it."

Whistler's Mother

Our house is always open to our friends and family. They pop in any time, no special occasion necessary, and I love that. The other day some friends surprised us and came over just to say hi. I was sitting in the family room with them. They both started laughing. When I asked why, they said "listen." "What do you hear?" I asked. "Happiness" they responded as they listened to my husband in his office, singing, and my son in the kitchen, whistling. No special reason, just happy.

"I'm singing in the rain. What a glorious feeling I'm happy again"

Can't say Don't

There are times that a big vocabulary can be impressive. You'll be "happy" to know I am suggesting you eliminate certain words. Your words represent your thoughts. Your actions are reactions to those thoughts and words. So, train your mind that you don't say can't, can't say don't and never say never.

"YOU CAN CHANGE YOUR WORLD BY CHANGING YOUR WORDS"

"Adversity is a fact of life. It can't be controlled. What we can control is how we react to it."

Lights, Camera, Action

When my company was nominated for a major industry award, news cameras came to my home to film "a day in the life." Minutes before the television crew was expected to arrive, one of our toilets overflowed. Luckily we have a live in plumber. (kidding). We *were* able to get things cleaned and fixed just in time, but as you can imagine it made for a less than relaxing start of the day. Happiness isn't about perfection. It is in the way you see things. The show must go on. You choose... Comedy or a drama.

The airplane takes off against the wind, not with it.

Security!

I was invited to attend a very foo foo wedding. By that I mean the bride and groom pulled out all the stops to make their special day quite an event. In fact, the special day was several days of festivities. Several celebrities and superstar athletes were in attendance. It took place at a secluded beach location. I needed to carefully plan what I packed because it really was a secluded location with no place to easily pick up something I may have forgotten. I arrived, put on my new beach dress and headed to the party. Something just didn't feel right but I couldn't put my finger on it. I felt like people were staring at me - but not in the way I might want. None the less, I proceeded to an empty chair and relaxed...in my new beach dress (did I mention that?).

A woman approached me and, seemingly embarrassed for me, said "Excuse me, you have something on your dress." I am no stranger to spilling things on my clothes, so I wasn't too concerned until I looked down and saw a tag. No, not the kind you can cut off. The big, heavy anti-theft bar. It was hanging from my beach dress! I had a few options. I could go to my hotel room and miss the party. Not really an option. I could forgot the cover up and just wear my swimsuit. Again, not really an option. (I prefer my sweater body to my bathing suit body). Or, I could accept it and not let it interfere with having a fun time. Bingo!

Go Ahead, Use the Soap

I was having a conversation with a woman sitting next to me on a plane. She owns a gift store. I asked her about some of the products she sells and she told me about one of her favorite items. A bar of soap. She described why this soap was special. It smelled like nothing she ever smelled before. I could see she was happy just talking about it. Then she told me she never used hers. "Why not?" I asked. "I'm saving it." Saving a bar of soap? "Is it hard to get?" I asked. "No" she said. "Is it very expensive?" "No" she said. "I'm just waiting for a special day." Every day is special. Go ahead, use the soap.

"The only thing that happens when you wait is that you get older"

If the Chew Fits….

Many years ago I needed to pick something up at the mall. My husband came along to keep me company. We passed a high end department store, and something caught my eye. There was a pair of shoes that was so stunning I was drawn to it. My husband noticed me staring and suggested I try them on. "OK" I said. No arm twisting necessary here. They were comfortable *and* beautiful…but expensive. I decided to treat myself. About a week later we got another treat….a puppy. She was so cute and cuddly. The puppy was so well behaved, except for one little incident. We still don't know when, why or how…but she found my expensive, beautiful new shoes and enjoyed them much more than she did any toy or milk bone. She devoured the shoes. I wasn't happy. That was the only time she ever did anything like that. We treasured that dog and spent 14 wonderful years together. The love we had for that dog and the fun times we spent together far outweigh the one unhappy memory of her eating my favorite shoes. Don't let one incident stand in the way of your happiness. After the serious shoe chewing it would have been easy to label the puppy as mischievous and expect her to continue acting out, claiming that was her nature. The way you treat people (and puppies) has a direct impact on their actions. By controlling the way you see things, you control your happiness.

"The world is a great mirror. It reflects back to you what you are. If you are loving, if you are friendly, if you are helpful, the world will prove loving and friendly and helpful to you. The world is what you are." Thomas Dreier

"One of the most rewarding moments in life is when you finally find the courage to let go of what you can't change"

Let it Go

I know a woman in her late eighties. Through the years she has accumulated quite a few things. It is not her jewelry or silver that she is attached to, but rather a fish plate. Yes, a plate with a picture of a fish. There is no monetary or sentimental value that I know of, just something she likes...a lot. There used to be two fish plates. One day her son had a friend over. They were playing in her apartment, the friend threw a ball, the woman's son didn't catch it, and bye bye fish plate. The "boy" is now a full grown adult receiving social security. He is a wonderful and devoted son. His mother continues to remind him how he missed the ball causing the plate to break. ...in 1954. To be happy, you need to know when to let things go.

I Remember it Well

I was in a hospital bed. My family was in the waiting room. A nurse was constantly at my side. The pain was intense. Then I heard a baby cry. It was the happiest day of my life. My son was born.

"The two most important days in your life are the day you are born and the day you find out why."

Mark Twain

You can be or do anything.
Including be happy.

It is your choice.

Choose Happy

"The only person you are destined to become is the person you decide to be"